Two-Fisted Science

First Printing
ISBN 0-9660106-0-4

All stories ©1996, 1997 Jim Ottaviani. Artwork ©1996, 1997 Mark Badger, Donna Barr, Sean Bieri, Paul Chadwick, Guy Davis, Colleen Doran, David Lasky, Steve Lieber, Lin Lucas, Bernie Mireault, Scott Roberts, Scott Saavedra, and Rob Walton.

SCIENCE FICTION

Though this is fictionalized science, it's not science fiction.
We've imagined some of the details, but the characters existed,
and did and said (most of) the things you'll read.

Two-Fisted Science is published with the generous assistance of the Xeric Foundation. Thanks also to Ralph Leighton, Tom Van Sant, and Danny Hillis for granting permission to adapt their Feynman stories. You can catch Gemstone Publishing in the midst of reprinting similarly named 1950s EC comics at your local comic book store. Though I like *Two-Fisted Tales*, *Weird Science*, *Weird Fantasy*, and *Frontline Combat* best, every title features art and storytelling lessons masquerading as entertaining comics. No portion of this book may be reproduced by any means, except for purposes of review, without the express written consent of Jim Ottaviani at 315 W. Davis, Ann Arbor, MI 48103 or Two-Fisted_Science@umich.edu.　　　　A GENERAL TEXTRONICS LABS production.

TABLE of CONTENTS

prologue

Art: Donna Barr ©1996

TWO-FISTED

IN 1054, ROUGHLY 500 YEARS BEFORE GALILEO GALILEI WAS BORN, A SUPERNOVA APPEARED. WE CALL IT THE CRAB NEBULA, AND TODAY IT'S HARD TO SEE WITH THE NAKED EYE. BUT AT ITS PEAK, IT WAS SO BRIGHT THAT PEOPLE SAW IT IN BROAD DAYLIGHT, AND EVERYDAY ASTRONOMERS WATCHED IT MAKE A

FULL CIRCLE

OVERHEAD

I, IBN BUTLAN, NOTE THIS SPECTACULAR STAR APPEARING IN GEMINI THIS YEAR - 446. MAY ALLAH WILL THAT WE SURVIVE THIS CALAMITY.

I humbly observe that a guest star has appeared to the south-east of Tien-Kuan, this fifth month of the first year of the Chih-Ho reign period.

ASTRONOMERS IN PERSIA AND CATHAY STUDIED THIS AMAZING OCCURRENCE — SO BRIGHT THEY COULD SEE IT NIGHT AND DAY. THEIR OBSERVATIONS ARE SOME OF THE MOST DETAILED AND WONDERFUL IN SCIENCE HISTORY.

A.D. 1564

WAAAA

MADONNA! THIS ONE'S GONNA BE TROUBLE...

ART BY SCOTT ROBERTS

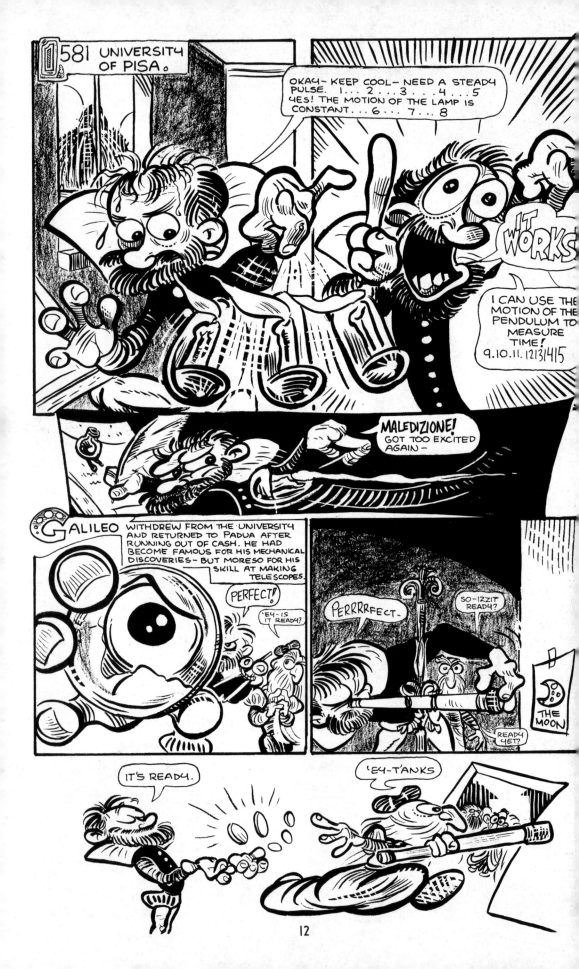

GALILEO MADE MANY OBSERVATIONS WITH HIS TELESCOPES~

IDIOTS! LOOKING AT WARSHIPS, WHEN THEY COULD BE SEEING THIS— THE SURFACE OF THE MOON!

FOUR MOONS!*

* THERE WERE ACTUALLY SIXTEEN MOONS, BUT GALILEO'S TELESCOPES WEREN'T *THAT* GOOD.

?!

...AND THE MILKY WAY— COMPOSED OF THOUSANDS OF STARS!

1632 THE Vatican

YOU USED MY CONCLUSION FOR "Dialogue Concerning the Two Chief World Systems"

HAVEN'T READ IT ALL THE WAY THROUGH YET MYSELF BUT MY ADVISOR'S SAY DISTURBING THINGS ABOUT IT. YOU'VE CAST YOURSELF AS SALVIATI—YES?

UH—YEAH

AND THE INTELLIGENT LAYMAN IS SAGREDO? AND The Church IS THE *FOOL*, SIMPLICIO?

UH—YEAH.

KINDA—

AND SIMPLICIO'S ARGUMENTS ARE REFUTED *ALL THE WAY THROUGH*? AND I'VE GOT A DOCUMENT HERE FROM 1616, WRITTEN BY CARDINAL BELLARMINE—FORBIDDING YOU TO "TEACH OR DISCUSS COPERNICANISM IN ANY WAY". WHICH YOU HAVE CONVENIENTLY MISPLACED? CAN YOU DENY THAT The Church IS CAST AS SIMPLICIO? OR THAT YOU DON'T HAVE BELLARMINE'S WRIT?

UM—NO GUESS NOT.

LOOK. THE JESUITS TELL ME THAT YOUR BOOK MIGHT HAVE WORSE CONSEQUENCES THAN LUTHER AND CALVIN PUT TOGETHER.

SO. WHAT CAN I DO? MY HANDS ARE TIED. FORTUNATELY— CARDINALS ZACCHIA, BARBERINI, AND BORGIA ABSTAINED—SO I DON'T HAVE TO EXCOMMUNICATE YOU. EVEN THOUGH THE CONGREGATION WOULD JUST *LOVE* THAT.

RECANT. GO HOME. DO SOME··· WHAT DO YOU CALL THEM···· EXPERIMENTS. *BUT DON'T MESS WITH THE SUN ANYMORE.*

OKAY?

GALILEO?

LIGHT MUST BE PRETTY DAMN FAST, SAGREDO. WE SEE LIGHTNING BEFORE WE HEAR IT. AND WE KNOW SOUND MOVES QUICKLY BETWEEN US.

AN EXPERIMENT: TWO GUYS EACH HOLD A LANTERN. FACING EACH OTHER THEY REVEAL AND CONCEAL THE LIGHT, SO THAT WHEN ONE SAW THE OTHER'S, HE'D UNCOVER HIS. DOING THE EXPERIMENT AT VARIOUS DISTANCES, IF THE REPLIES TOOK THE SAME TIME WHEN CLOSE AS WHEN THEY WERE FAR AWAY, WE COULD CONCLUDE THAT LIGHT TRAVELS INSTANTANEOUSLY!

THE EXPERIMENT SEEMS BOTH SURE AND INGENIOUS. WHAT DID YOU CONCLUDE FROM IT?

ACTUALLY, I DIDN'T TRY IT, EXCEPT AT A SMALL DISTANCE. I CAN'T GO FAR FROM HERE, OLD FRIEND— SO I COULDN'T TELL.

BUT IN WHAT SEAS AM I ENGULFING YOU? VOIDS—INFINITES—INDIVISIBLES, AND INSTANTANEOUS MOVEMENTS. GOD KNOWS, THEY'VE CAUSED ME TROUBLE.

BEAUTIFUL, THOUGH

EUROPEAN RECORDS MAKE NO MENTION THE AGE WASN'T DA BECAUSE NO LIGHTS SHONE —

BUT BECAUSE NO O LOOKED AT THE LIGH THERE FOR EVERYON TO SEE.

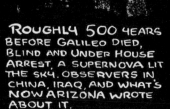

ROUGHLY 500 YEARS BEFORE GALILEO DIED, BLIND AND UNDER HOUSE ARREST, A SUPERNOVA LIT THE SKY. OBSERVERS IN CHINA, IRAQ, AND WHAT'S NOW ARIZONA WROTE ABOUT IT.

IN 1992 - 350 YE, AFTER GALILEO'S DEATH, THE CATHOLIC CHURC OFFICIALLY APOLOGIZED FOR CENSURING HIM

In 1676, before ISAAC NEWTON and ROBERT HOOKE became enemies (the former asserted that light was made of particles, the latter that it was made of waves) Newton wrote to the renowned microscopist, saying: "If I have seen further than other men, it is because I stood on THE SHOULDERS OF GIANTS

Newton

Leibniz

HEY ISAAC!

Pils

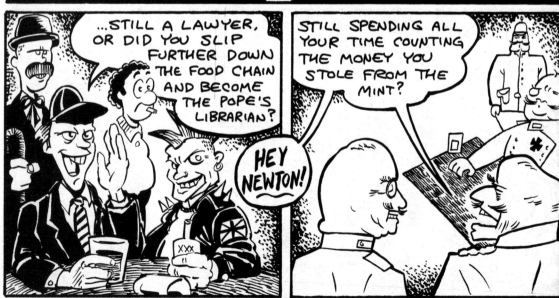

YOU SHOULD TALK! STILL SPENDING YOUR TIME ON **GENEOLOGY** TO HELP SEMI-ROYAL BASTARDS INHERIT MONEY THAT THEY NEGLECTED TO... TO FORNICATE THEMSELVES INTO?

YOU SHOULD TALK! STILL BEATING UP CHILDREN AT YOUR SO-CALLED CHURCH AND HANGING AROUND WITH LITTLE GIRLS?

LAWYER!!

POLITICIAN!

VAS IST DER PROBLEM?

DUNNO, MATE. NEVER MESS WITH POLITICS, MESELF.

POUR US ANOTHER, THERE'S A GOOD CHAP.

EPILOGUE:

NEWTON HAD A GOOD LIFE, EXCELLING AND PROSPERING AT THE MINT. IN HIS LATER YEARS HE BECAME A BIT OF A POLITICAL HACK AND DIDN'T DO MUCH OF INTEREST INTELLECTUALLY BESIDES SOLVING TWO OF LEIBNIZ'S MATHEMATICAL CHALLENGES. BOTH TIMES HE HEARD OF THEM AFTER A HARD DAY AT THE OFFICE AND SOLVED THEM OVER DINNER.

LEIBNIZ ENDED UP DESTITUTE, TOSSED ASIDE BY HIS ARISTOCRATIC SPONSORS WHEN THEY NO LONGER NEEDED HIS LEGAL SKILLS. ON THE BRIGHT SIDE, WE STILL WRITE CALCULUS HIS WAY. THE BRITISH, ON THE OTHER HAND, ROTTED MATHEMATICALLY FOR AT LEAST A CENTURY, COMPELLED BY NATIONAL PRIDE TO USE NEWTON'S INFERIOR NOTATION.

I do not know what I may appear to the world, but to myself I seem to have been only like a boy playing on the seashore, and diverting myself now and then finding a smoother pebble or a prettier shell than ordinary, whilst the great ocean of truth lay all undiscovered before me.

— Isaac Newton, from Brewster's *Memoirs of Newton*.

WHAT HAPPENED?!

SHHHH!

WHAT?

SOMEONE JUST TRIED TO GET INTO BUILDING OMEGA...

I SCARED HIM OFF!

SAFECRACKER

PART ONE:
A VERY GOOD SCHEME.

LEO LAVATELLI TAUGHT ME HOW TO PICK LOCKS.

CLICK CLICK

SOMETIMES YOU SLIP, AND HAVE TO START OVER AGAIN.

CLICK CLICK

IT'S LIKE SISYPHUS: YOU'RE ALWAYS FALLING DOWN HILL.

HEY LOOK! I DON'T EVEN HAVE TO PICK THE LOCK!

FINALLY, SOME CABINETS WITH COMBINATION LOCKS CAME FROM THE MOSLER SAFE COMPANY.

NOW THAT'S A FILING CABINET! I HOPE I GET ONE!

THEY WERE AN IMMEDIATE CHALLENGE.

HAVING TROUBLE, FEYNMAN?

I LOVE PUZZLES, SO I TOOK APART THE ONE IN MY OFFICE.

I DIDN'T GET ANYWHERE, SO I BOUGHT SOME BOOKS BY SAFECRACKERS.

THEY WERE ALL THE SAME.

IN THE FIRST PART THEY TOLD STORIES OF THEIR FANTASTIC ACHIEVEMENTS.

IN THE SECOND PART, THEY TOLD YOU HOW.

NINNY-PINNY, DOPEY THINGS.

"THINK OF THE PSYCHOLOGY OF THE OWNER."

"LOTS OF PEOPLE LIKE TO USE DATES FOR COMBINATIONS."

"THE SECRETARY MIGHT WRITE IT DOWN IN ONE OF THE FOLLOWING PLACES..."

THEY COULDN'T HAVE OPENED SAFES AT ANY SPEED WITH THAT CRAP.

I WENT BACK TO MY OWN STUDIES.

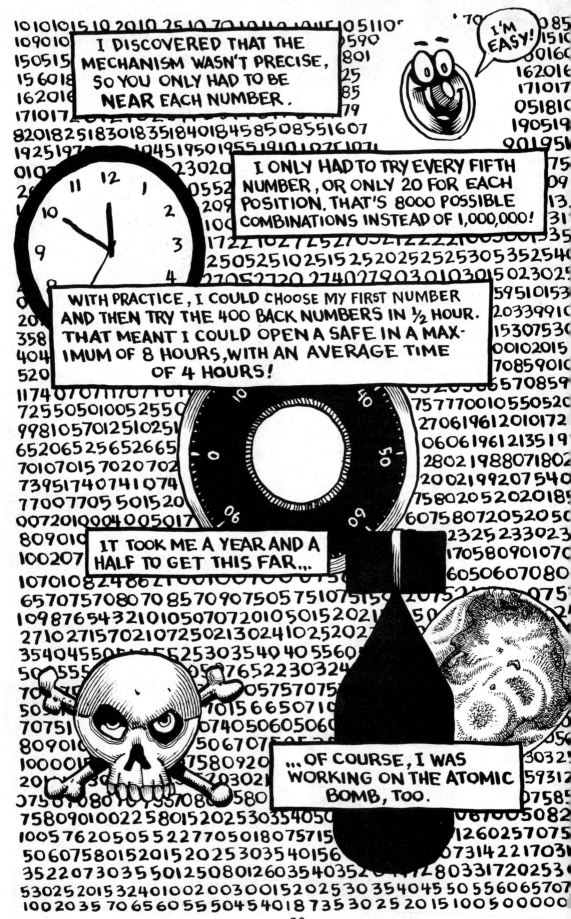

I DISCOVERED THAT THE MECHANISM WASN'T PRECISE, SO YOU ONLY HAD TO BE NEAR EACH NUMBER.

I'M EASY!

I ONLY HAD TO TRY EVERY FIFTH NUMBER, OR ONLY 20 FOR EACH POSITION. THAT'S 8000 POSSIBLE COMBINATIONS INSTEAD OF 1,000,000!

WITH PRACTICE, I COULD CHOOSE MY FIRST NUMBER AND THEN TRY THE 400 BACK NUMBERS IN ½ HOUR. THAT MEANT I COULD OPEN A SAFE IN A MAXIMUM OF 8 HOURS, WITH AN AVERAGE TIME OF 4 HOURS!

IT TOOK ME A YEAR AND A HALF TO GET THIS FAR...

... OF COURSE, I WAS WORKING ON THE ATOMIC BOMB, TOO.

32

HOLY COW! HE DID IT!

I SEE WHAT YOU MEAN. IT'S A VERY GOOD SCHEME.

T WAS PURE LUCK, BUT I PRETENDED IT WAS NO BIG DEAL, AND STALEY PLAYED ALONG.

MY REPUTATION AS A SAFECRACKER BORDERED ON THE SUPERNATURAL AFTER THAT.

Notes and References

A Night Before

Like the woman at the end of the pier, we don't know what Pauli was really thinking about that night — either before or after she interrupted his train of thought (and perhaps changed its track). But we do know that this scene occurred, thanks to Jeremy Bernstein's book *Hans Bethe, Prophet of Energy* (NY: Basic Books, 1980).

> For me in any case it is much too difficult, and I wish I were a film comedian or something similar and had never heard of physics.
> — Pauli, quoted in *Uncertainty*, by David Cassidy, (NY: W.H. Freeman, 1991). Charlie Chaplin was all the rage in Copenhagen in the 1920s.

Full Circle

Heavy-handed repression of science by a religious bureaucracy might seem odd and antiquated. If you have to deal with school boards telling you to teach creationism on the same footing as evolution you probably don't find it so quaint.

> *Two New Sciences*, Galileo Galilei as translated by Stillman Drake, (Toronto: Wall & Thompson, 2nd edition, 1989). Tough going, so skip right to his experiment to test whether light travels instantaneously.

> *Space*, by James Michener, (NY: Ballantine, 1982). This novel gave me my first exposure to the story of the 1054 supernova.

> *The World of Physics*, by Jefferson H. Weaver, (NY: Simon and Schuster, 1987). Gives excerpts from Galileo's "Dialogue Concerning the Two Chief World Systems".

> *Supernovae*, by Paul & Lesley Murdin, (Cambridge: Cambridge University Press, 1978). Ibn Butlan's description comes from this book, which also discusses ancient cultures' constellations and observation methods.

> *Galileo, Science and the Church*, by Jerome Langsford, (Ann Arbor: The University of Michigan Press, 3rd edition, 1992). Very dry, but an essential source for details on Galileo's trial.

Shoulders of Giants

Though they never confronted each other in person (and wouldn't have done it in a pub or Biergarten if they had), Newton and Leibniz did little to discourage their compatriots from attacking each other's character.

> *Men of Mathematics*, by E.T. Bell, (NY: Dover, 1937). An extremely engaging book. Bell is in turns gossipy and informative and entertaining, especially where Newton's and Leibniz' lives are concerned.

The Nature and Growth of Mathematics, by Edna E. Kramer, (Princeton: Princeton University Press, 1970). The intellectual history of math, including calculus and the paths Newton and Leibniz used to get to it.

Principia Mathematica, by Isaac Newton, 1672. A real page-turner, and the source for all the Latin stuff that fooled you into thinking that Sean and I are very learned.

The World of Physics, by Jefferson Hane Weaver, (NY: Simon and Schuster, 1987). Weaver traces the background of the dispute and the agendas of the learned societies that fueled it.

A Very Good Scheme

More on Feynman appears in the next set of notes, but if you're impatient to get to the source material for the safecracker story, refer to:

"Surely you're joking, Mr. Feynman!", by Richard Feynman, as told to Ralph Leighton, (NY: W.W. Norton, 1985) and *Safecracker Suite* , sound recording by Ralph Leighton, 1988.

Artists

Donna Barr writes and draws *The Desert Peach* and *Stinz*, available from MU/Aeon Press.

Sean Bieri writes and draws *Cool Jerk and Homogal, Jape,* and other mini-comics available directly from his own Garlic Press.

Bernie Mireault writes and draws *The Jam*, available from Caliber, has worked in the Batman, Grendel, and "Classics Desecrated" milieus, and is probably working on his new series or coloring for DC and Dark Horse right now.

Scott Roberts writes and draws *Patty Cake*, available from the spunky crew at Slave Labor Graphics.

Once, after a thoroughly stupid Tom Mix film, [Bohr's] verdict went about as follows: "I did not like the picture; it was too improbable. That the scoundrel runs off with the beautiful girl is logical; it always happens. That the bridge collapses under their carriage is unlikely, but I am willing to accept it. That the heroine remains suspended in mid-air over a precipice is even more unlikely, but again I accept it. I am even willing to accept that at that very moment Tom Mix is coming by on his horse. But that at that very moment there should be a fellow with a motion picture camera to film the whole business — that is more than I am willing to believe."
    — H.B.G. Casimir, from "Recollections from the Years 1929–1931".

FEYNMAN

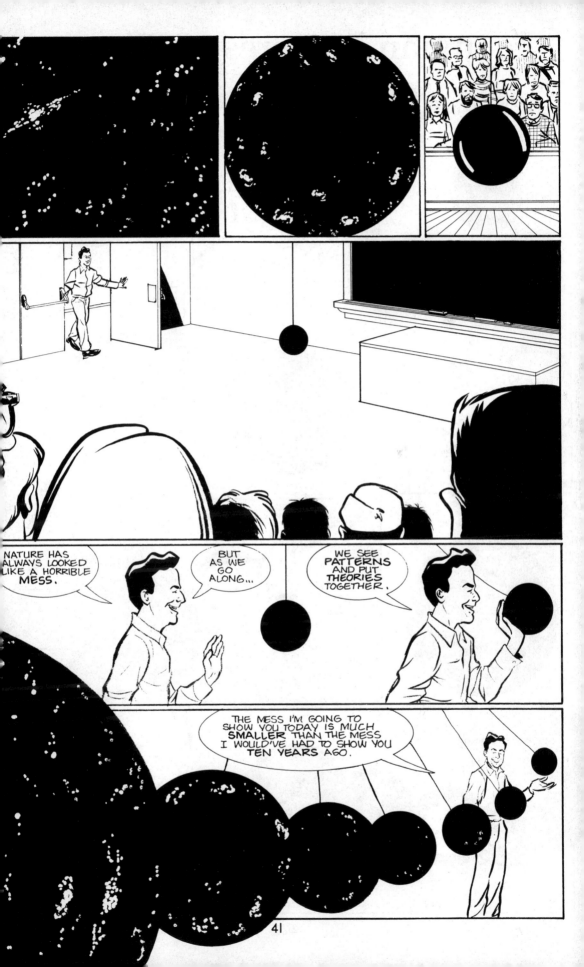

Feynman Lectures on Physics

AND THINK ABOUT THE **MESS** AT THE BEGINNING OF THIS CENTURY, BEFORE QUANTUM MECHANICS!

THERE WAS HEAT, MAGNETISM, ELECTRICITY, LIGHT, X-RAYS, AND **ON** AND **ON**.

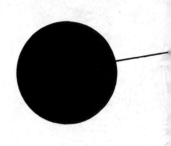

CLASSICAL PHYSICS COULDN'T HANDLE ANY OF IT.

BUT I'M **ALSO** GOING TO SHOW THAT DIFFERENT THEORIES OF PHYSICS ARE VERY SIMILAR.

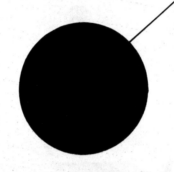

MAYBE BECAUSE OF OUR LIMITED **IMAGINATION**.

WE TRY FITTING EVERY NEW PHENOMENON INTO THE FRAMEWORK WE ALREADY HAVE.

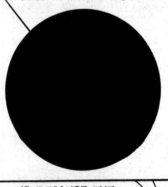

SO WHEN SOME **FOOL** PHYSICIST GIVES A LECTURE ON QUANTUM PHYSICS AND SAYS:

"THIS IS THE WAY IT WORKS, AND LOOK HOW WONDERFULLY SIMILAR ALL OUR THEORIES ARE..."

IT'S **NOT** BECAUSE NATURE IS REALLY SIMILAR.

IT'S BECAUSE THE PHYSICISTS HAVE ONLY BEEN ABLE TO THINK OF THE **SAME DAMN** THING OVER AND OVER AGAIN.

I have a friend who's an artist, and he sometimes takes a view which I don't agree with. He'll hold up a flower and say, "Look how beautiful it is," and I'll agree. But then he'll say, "I, as an artist, can see how beautiful a flower is. But you, as a scientist, take it all apart and it becomes dull." I think he's kind of nutty. First of all, the beauty that he sees is available to other people — and to me, too, I believe... But at the same time, I see much more of the flower than he sees. I can imagine the cells inside, which also have a beauty. There's beauty not just at the dimension of one centimeter; there's also beauty at a smaller dimension... It only adds. I don't understand how it subtracts.

— Richard Feynman, from *"What do you care what other people think?"*.

Arline

I'm sitting on a couch with my arm around a girl, practicing a new art (an older guy had just given me a demonstration of it with his girlfriend), when someone says:

SHE'S HERE! SHE'S HERE!

She was very pretty, but I did believe in this undemocratic business of changing what yo doing just because the que comes in.

The first time I ever said anything to her was at a dance. I always had problems cutting in. When a girl's near you, you think "Well, no, this isn't my kind of music". So you wait.

When the music changes, yo sort of step forward, or at le you think you do, when so other guy cuts in front of

After some fooling around, I finally muttered something to the guy next to me.

HEY, LISTEN TO THIS: FEYNMAN WANTS TO DANCE WITH ARLINE!

Soon one of the guys I hung around with is dancing with her. They ended up near us, and I finally did it.

We only danced for a few m utes before someone else cut

...ater, I invited her to one of these dances—the first time I took her out. My mother invited my best friends, too, to get more customers for her friend's dance studio.

LISTEN FEYNMAN—WE WANT YOU TO UNDERSTAND THAT WE UNDERSTAND THAT ARLINE'S YOUR GIRL TONIGHT.

WE'RE NOT GOING TO BOTHER HER.

SHE'S OUT OF BOUNDS FOR US.

But before long, precisely these guys were cutting in and competing with me.

SO THAT'S WHAT "METHINKS THOU DOST PROTEST TOO MUCH" MEANS!

She was in the art group at the Jewish youth center. I had no interest in any subject except science, but I joined too... I struggled, learning how to make plaster casts of faces (which I've since used, as it turned out), just so I could be in the group... But her boyfriend was there too, so I had no chance.

But one day she told me he wasn't her boyfriend anymore. That was the beginning of **hope!**

The first time I went over, the porch wasn't lit. I didn't want to disturb anyone by asking if it was the right house.

15 4

1...
5...
4...

She was having trouble with her philosophy homework.

HE STARTS WITH "COGITO, ERGO SUM" AND ENDS UP PROVING THE EXISTENCE of GOD.

IMPOSSIBLE!

Even though I doubted the great Descartes, I tried to follow it through.

WELL, HE KNOWS DOUBT EXISTS, AND IF HIS THOUGHTS ARE IMPERFECT, THEN HE KNOWS PERFECTION MUST EXIST TOO.

THAT DOESN'T PROVE ANYTHING. IN SCIENCE WE TALK ABOUT RELATIVE APPROXIMATIONS WITHOUT HAVING A PERFECT THEORY.

She understood that no matter how impressive and important philosophy was supposed to be, it could be taken lightly.

At least by me.

WELL, I GUESS IT'S OKAY TO TAKE THE OTHER SIDE.

MY TEACHER SAYS "THERE ARE TWO SIDES TO EVERY QUESTION, JUST LIKE THERE ARE TWO SIDES TO EVERY PIECE OF PAPER."

Gotcha!

THERE'S TWO SIDES TO THAT, TOO.

WHAT DO YOU MEAN?

I had read about Möbius strips in the Britannica. (People didn't know much about these things then.) A one-sided surface wasn't some wishy-washy political question, or something you needed history to understand.

TAKE A PIECE of PAPER, and PUT A HALF-TWIST IN IT.

MÖBIUS, AUGUST FERDINAND astronomer and mathematician, was bo... of November 1790. At Leipzig... four years, ultimately d... In 1815 he s...

MAKE A LOOP OF IT AND YOU HAVE A ONE-SIDED SURFACE.

The next day in class she lay in wait for her teacher. Sure enough...

THERE ARE TWO SIDES TO EVERY QUESTION, JUST AS THERE ARE TWO SIDES TO EVERY PIECE OF PAPER.

THERE AREN'T EVEN TWO SIDES TO THAT!

I think she paid more attention to me after that.

We began to mold each other's personalities. Her family was very polite, so she taught me to be more sensitive to other people's feelings.

I thought one should have the attitude of "What do you care what other people think?"

WE SHOULD LISTEN TO OTHER PEOPLE'S OPINIONS AND TAKE THEM INTO ACCOUNT...

BUT IF THEY DON'T MAKE SENSE AND WE THINK THEY'RE WRONG, THEN THAT'S THAT!

She caught on right away. We were very honest with each other, and it worked well.

WE BECAME VERY MUCH IN LOVE-- A LOVE LIKE NO OTHER THAT I KNOW OF...

After that summer, I went away to MIT. (I couldn't go to Columbia because of the Jewish quota ✱.) My friends sent me letters saying things like, "You should see who she's going out with," or "She's doing this and that while you're all alone up in Boston." I was taking out other girls. They didn't mean a thing, and I know the same was true for her.

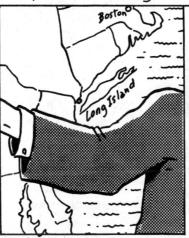

Boston
Long Island

I stayed in Boston that summer, and she found a job nearby. We only saw each other a couple of times, though.

My father was concerned that I would become too involved with her and get off track in my studies.

So he talked me, or her (I don't remember) out of getting married. Those days were very, very different from now.

✱ THE QUOTA SYSTEM LIMITED THE NUMBER OF PLACES AVAILABLE TO JEWISH STUDENTS.

After I graduated from MIT, I went to Princeton. When I came home one time she had developed a bump on her neck. It worried us a little bit.

IT DOESN'T HURT.

RUB IT WITH SOME OMEGA OIL* AND IT'LL GO AWAY.

Sometime later the bump got bigger -- or maybe it was smaller -- and the hospital said she had typhoid fever. Right away I researched it.

The next time I visited, I asked the doctor how the Wydell test came out.

NEGATIVE.

WHAT? HOW CAN THAT BE? WHY ALL THESE GOWNS, THEN?

MAYBE SHE DOESN'T HAVE TYPHOID FEVER!

The result was that the doctor talked to her parents, who told me not to interfere.

AFTER ALL, HE'S THE DOCTOR. YOU'RE ONLY HER "FIANCÉ".

Anyway, after a little while she got better, apparently. The swelling went down and the fever went away. But later it started again. This time the doctor noticed swelling in her armpits and groin.

As soon as I heard about it, I went down to the library at Princeton to look up lymphatic diseases.

I find "Swelling of the Lymphatic Glands." "(1) TUBERCULOSIS of the LYMPHATIC GLANDS. THIS IS VERY EASY TO DIAGNOSE."

THIS ISN'T WHAT SHE HAS, BECAUSE THE DOCTORS ARE HAVING TROUBLE FIGURING IT OUT.

SO I started reading about some other diseases Lymphodenema, Lympho-denoma, Hodgkin's Disease, and all kinds of other things:

* OMEGA OIL WAS A POPULAR REMEDY FOR BITES and RASHES.

I decided the most likely possibility was an incurable disease. Then I went to the weekly tea at Palmer Hall to talk with the mathematicians.

It was very strange — like **I** had **two** minds.

When I went to visit, I told the joke about people who don't know anything about medicine reading things and assuming they have a fatal disease.

I said I also thought that we were in great difficulty, and that one of the diseases she might have was Hodgkin's.

When she next saw her doctor, she asked about it.

COULD IT BE HODGKIN'S DISEASE?

WELL, YES, THAT'S A POSSIBILITY.

When she went to the county hospital, the doctor wrote: "Hodgkin's disease—?"

THE DOCTOR DOESN'T KNOW ANY MORE THAN I DO ABOUT THIS.

They ran all sorts of tests for this "Hodgkin's disease—?" and held special meetings to discuss this peculiar case. I remember waiting for her outside once, when...

TELL ME, HAVE YOU EVER COUGHED UP BLOOD?

GO AWAY!

WHAT KIND OF THING IS THAT TO ASK OF A PATIENT?

...

I didn't catch on. He was checking something, and if I'd been smart, I would have asked him what it was.

Finally, after a lot of discussion, a doctor told me they figure the most likely possibility is Hodgkin's.

THERE WILL BE SOME PERIODS of IMPROVEMENT and SOME PERIODS IN THE HOSPITAL.

THERE'S NO WAY TO REVERSE IT ENTIRELY.

I'M SORRY TO HEAR THAT. I'LL TELL HER WHAT YOU SAID.

NO, NO! WE DON'T WANT T UPSET THE PATIENT!

NO! WE'VE ALREADY DISCUSSED THE POSSIBILITY. I KNOW SHE CAN ADJUST TO IT.

HER PARENTS DON'T WANT HER TO KNOW. YOU HAD BETTER ASK THEM FIRST.

At home, everybody worked on me: my parents, my aunts, our family doctor. Everybody said I was wrong. I thought I was definitely right.

HOW COULD YOU DO SUCH A TERRIBLE THING!

WHAT COULD YOU BE THINKING?

THAT'S CHILDISH

BLAH BLAH BLAH

BLAH BLAH.

BLAH BLAH

WHAT WERE

BLAH BLAH

BLAH BLAH

WE MADE A PACT.

THERE'S NO FOOLING AROUND. SHE'S GONNA ASK ME WHAT SHE'S GOT, AND I CAN'T LIE TO HER.

But finally my little sister ran up to me.

SHE'S SO WONDERFUL AND YOU'RE SO STUBBORN!

I couldn't take it any more. That broke me down. So I wrote her a good-bye love letter, figuring that if she ever found out the truth, we would be through. I carried it with me all the time.

THEY'RE TELLING ME I HAVE GLANDULAR FEVER, AND I'M NOT SURE WHETHER TO BELIEVE THEM.

TELL ME, RICHARD, DO I HAVE HODGKIN'S DISEASE?

YOU HAVE GLANDULAR FEVER.

And I died inside...

So we knew we could face things together, and after going through that we had no difficulty facing other problems. My family started working on me again. But since they had given me this kind of advice before, and had been so wrong, I was in a muc[h] stronger position.

BUT YOU'LL GET SICK, TOO!

LOOK, IT'S NOT A REAL PROMISE. YOU MADE IT WHEN YOU DIDN'T KNOW THE SITUATION.

WE ALREADY KNOW NOT TO KISS.

AND WOULD IT BE SENSIBLE FOR A HUSBAND WHO LEARNS THAT HIS WIFE IS SICK TO LEAVE HER?

We worked everything out. We got married on the way to Deborah Hospital, which is near Princeton.

The guy in the borough of Richmond's city hall was very nice-- he did everything right away.

YOU DON'T HAVE ANY WITNESSES.

HEY GUYS, COME IN HERE!

—We were very happy.

YOU'RE MARRIED NOW.

YOU SHOULD KISS THE BRIDE!

So this bashful character did, and then we got back in the car and drove to the hospital.

54

...isited her there every ...ekend, but we wrote each ...her too. One time I re-...ived a box of pencils in the ...il. She'd had them engraved.

RICHARD DARLING, ...LOVE YOU! PUTSY"

Well, that was nice, and I love her too, but-- you know how you absentmindedly drop pencils around. You're showing Professor Wigner* a formula or something...

RICHARD DARLING, I L...

HA HA HA

...those days we didn't have ...tra stuff, so I didn't want ... waste them. And she ...ouldn't have to know.

ktch ktch

But the very next morning I got another letter...

WHAT'S THE IDEA of TRYING TO CUT THE NAME OFF of THE PENCILS?

WHAT DO YOU CARE WHAT OTHER PEOPLE THINK?

...e wrote a poem too. Each line ...ded with "Nuts to you" in a ...different form.

"IF YOU'RE ASHAMED OF ME, ...DAH DAH, THEN PECANS TO ...YOU! PECANS TO YOU!"

SO I HAD TO USE THEM. WHAT ELSE COULD I DO?

?

* Feynman's Ph.D. advisor (and Nobel Prize Winner) Eugene P. Wigner.

It wasn't long before I got recruited into the Manhattan Project. I went to Los Alamos and Robert Oppenheimer arranged for her to stay in Albuquerque. I got time off every weekend to visit.

I spent my weekdays studying and reading, studying and reading. The early days of the project were hectic, but that was lucky for me.

All the bigshots except for Hans Bethe were away, and Bethe needed someone to push his ideas against.

HEY DICK, C'MERE.

He would explain his theories.

...SO THAT'S WHY SEPARATING URANIUM WITH GASEOUS DIFFUSION IS BETTER THAN

NO, NO, YOU'RE CRAZY! IT'LL GO LIKE THIS!

...and I'd jump right in. You see, when I hear about physics, I just think about physics. I don't know who I'm talking to and say dopey things like "No, no, you're wrong."

JUST A MOMENT

YOU'VE MISUNDERSTOOD. IT MUST GO LIKE $1/r^2$...

But it turns out that's exactly what he needed. I got a notch up on account of that and ended up as a group leader under Bethe.

HOW ARE YOUR T4 GUYS DOING?

GREAT. I THINK THE METHOD WE CAME UP WITH WILL WORK FOR THE CRITICALITY PROBLEM.

IF WE CAN KEEP THOSE #@Z£%@ MECHANICAL CALCULATORS RUNNING.

BUT DON'T CHANGE THE SUBJECT. WHAT YOU SAID IS IMPOSSIBLE. YOU'RE MAD!

THERE THEY GO AGAIN.

And we would keep going like this. They called us the "Battleship" and the "Mosquito Boat."

The military censored our mail at Los Alamos. That's utterly illegal in the U.S., so they set up as a "voluntary" thing. We agreed not to seal our letters going out and let them open the ones coming in. We made up lots of rules, and they said they'd notify us if there were any difficulties. On the very first day...

WHAT'S THIS?

IT'S A LETTER FROM MY WIFE.

IT SAYS "JXYWZTW1X3". WHAT'S THAT?

A CODE.

WHAT'S THE KEY TO IT?

I DON'T KNOW.

YOU DON'T KNOW THE KEY?

WE HAVE A GAME. I CHALLENGE HER TO SEND ME A CODE I CAN'T DECIPHER, SEE?

WELL, YOU'LL HAVE TO TELL HER TO SEND THE KEY.

BUT I DON'T WANT TO SEE THE KEY.

ALL RIGHT. WE'LL TAKE THE KEY OUT.

We did that, but got in trouble anyway. The next day I got a letter saying "It's very difficult writing because I feel the ~~censor~~ looking over my shoulder."

HEY! YOU'RE NOT SUPPOSED TO TOUCH MY INCOMING MAIL!

DON'T BE RIDICULOUS! DO YOU THINK WE USE INK ERADICATORS? WE CUT THINGS OUT WITH SCISSORS.

As I found out, when I got the next letter. She had gotten me in trouble.

On purpose.

I didn't use the ink eradicator. It must have been the ~~censor~~.

There was a code included without the key so we removed it.

"THERE WAS A CODE INCLUDED WITHOUT THE KEY SO WE REMOVED IT."

When I went to see her that day, I found out she'd fooled us both.

WELL, WHERE'S ALL THE STUFF?

WHAT STUFF?

Again.

LITHARGE, GLYCERINE, HOT DOGS, LAUNDRY.

I WANTED TO MAKE CEMENT TO FIX MY ONYX BOX.

AND SOMETHING TO EAT.

Which reminds me: One time she sent me a big catalog. The censors didn't bother with it. But it confused the hell out of me.

IS SHE CRAZY? IT'S ALL OUT OF PROPORTION!

RANGE HOOD

50 GAL   100 GAL

Well, I'm trying to figure out what this big catalog for institutional kitchen equipment is leading to, when another one comes. And then another.

SHE'S WAY OUT OF SCALE!

I'M GOING TO HAVE TO WRITE HER THAT THIS IS TOO EXPENSIVE. SHE'S GOTTA BE REASONABLE.

RESTAURANT WORLD

When I got to Albuquerque the next Saturday, there's a little charcoal broiler in her room.

I THOUGHT WE COULD HAVE STEAKS.

BUT THIS HOSPITAL IS ON ROUTE 66, THE MAIN HIGHWAY ACROSS THE UNITED STATES!

I CAN'T DO THAT, WITH ALL THOSE CARS AND TRUCKS GOING BY!

WHAT DO YOU CARE WHAT OTHER PEOPLE THINK? ANYWAY, WE'LL COMPROMISE: YOU DON'T HAVE TO WEAR THE HAT and GLOVES.

TRY ON THE APRON.

BAR B-Q KING

Then there were the Christmas cards...

I CAN'T SEND THESE TO ENRICO FERMI and NIELS BOHR!

Merry Christmas From Rich and Putsy

WHAT DO YOU CARE WHAT OTHER PEOPLE THINK?

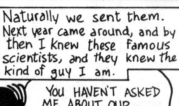

Naturally we sent them. Next year came around, and by then I knew these famous scientists, and they knew the kind of guy I am.

YOU HAVEN'T ASKED ME ABOUT OUR CHRISTMAS CARDS THIS YEAR, RICHARD...

She tortured me with "What do you care what other people think?" and my friends were happy she was having such a good time at my expense.

"Merry Christmas and a Happy New Year from Dr. & Mrs. R.P. Feynman."

WHAT'S WITH ALL THE FORMAL STUFF, DICK?

Actually, for security reasons we couldn't address the cards to "Bohr." His code name at Los Alamos was "Nicholas Baker." He picked me out at one of the meetings.

NO, IT'S NOT EFFICIENT! YOUR METHOD'S NOT GOING TO WORK!

His son Aage ("Jim Baker" during the war) told me why. His dad took him aside after that meeting.

REMEMBER THE NAME OF THAT LITTLE FELLOW BACK THERE. HE'S THE ONLY GUY WHO'S NOT AFRAID OF ME, and WILL SAY WHEN I'VE GOT A CRAZY IDEA.

NEXT TIME WE'LL TALK TO HIM BEFORE WE GET TO THESE GUYS WHO ONLY SAY "YES YES YES DR. BOHR".

So the next time he visited, he called me over first. We argued for hours.

HOW ABOUT SO and SO?

THAT SOUNDS A BIT BETTER, BUT IT'S GOT THIS DAMN FOOL IDEA IN IT!

And that's how it went. I was dumb that way, but it's the way I've always lived.

...nice if you can do it, and it goes well with my *Principle of* ...ial *Unresponsibility*. I learned that from Johnny.* On week-...s when I wasn't in Albuquerque we'd go for walks.

YOU DON'T HAVE TO BE RESPONSIBLE FOR THE WORLD YOU'RE IN.

That idea took me pretty far. Much later I was eating lunch at CERN with Victor Weiss-kopf. We put the principle to the test.

IN 10 YEARS TIME YOU'LL BE AN ADMINISTRATOR SUPERVISING PEOPLE WHOSE WORK YOU DON'T UNDERSTAND.

TEN BUCKS SAYS I WON'T!

I won that bet.

I learned more than just ...sics back then, especially on ...days. I didn't always ...e out on top, though. Once ...n I visited her she was ...cticing Chinese calligraphy. ...thought it was lovely, but...

...AT ONE'S ...RONG.

WHAT DO YOU MEAN "WRONG"? IT'S ONLY A HUMAN CONVENTION.

The great scientist knew that there's no law of nature that says how they're supposed to look.

I MEAN ARTISTICALLY IT'S WRONG. IT'S A QUESTION OF BALANCE. OF HOW IT FEELS.

BUT YOU CAN DO IT ANY WAY YOU WANT. ONE WAY IS JUST AS GOOD AS ANOTHER.

HERE.

MAKE ONE YOURSELF.

WAIT A MINUTE —

LET ME MAKE ANOTHER ONE... THIS ONE'S TOO BLOBBY.

HOW DO YOU KNOW HOW... BLOBBY... IT'S SUPPOSED TO BE?

I learned what she meant. An aesthetic thing has a certain character that I can't define. But she taught me there **is** something to it.

John von Neumann invented game theory and the modern computer.

59

Eventually, her condition became much weaker. So I arranged ahead of time with my friend Klaus* to borrow his car in case of an emergency.

YOU'D BETTER COME DOWN HERE RIGHT AWAY.

I picked up a couple of hitchhikers to help me in case something happened along the way.

When I got there, her father was so unhappy he had to leave. She was Fogged out.

I kept expecting an avalanche effect, with everything caving together in a dramatic collapse.

But she just slowly got mor Foggy, her breathing became less and less, until there was no more breath.

Her hair smelled exactly the san

* KLAUS FUCHS, WHO MADE VALUABLE CONTRIBUTIONS TO THE DEVELOPMENT OF THE BOMB, ALSO TURNED OUT TO BE A RUSSIAN SPY.

r me it was a kind of shock, cause in my mind something omentous had happened — d yet nothing had happened.

I didn't know how I was going to face my friends at Los Alamos. I didn't want people with long faces talking to me about death.

WHAT HAPPENED?

SHE'S DEAD.

AND HOW'S THE PROGRAM GOING?

They caught on right away.

must have done something o myself psychologically. didn't cry until about month later.

ARLINE WOULD LIKE THAT.

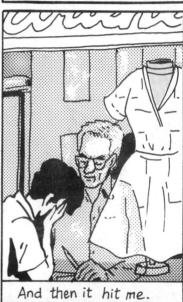

And then it hit me.

DARLING, I LOVE YOU!

SAFECRACKER

PART TWO:
EITHER YOU OPEN IT OR YOU DON'T.

NOW LIKE I SAID, WE WERE WORKING ON THE BOMB, SO I DIDN'T SPEND ALL MY TIME FOOLING AROUND WITH LOCKS.

BUT LIKE I ALSO SAID, AFTER A WHILE MY REPUTATION BEGAN TO SAIL...

HEY, FEYNMAN! CHRISTY'S OUT OF TOWN AND WE NEED A DOCUMENT FROM HIS SAFE.

CAN YOU OPEN IT?

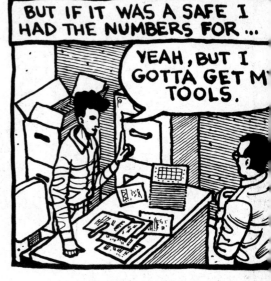

ONE DAY I HAD TO GO TO **OAK RIDGE, TENNESSEE**. I HAD WRITTEN A REPORT THAT HAD TO BE OKed BY A COLONEL, AN IMPORTANT GUY...

...WITH A MUCH **FANCIER** SAFE THAN EVERYBODY ELSE.

MIND IF I LOOK AT YOUR SAFE?

NOT AT ALL.

IT WAS OPEN. WHEN A SAFE IS OPEN, IT'S EASY TO GET THE LAST TWO NUMBERS OF THE COMBINATION IF YOU KNOW WHAT YOU'RE DOING.

I SAW THAT UNDERNEATH ALL THAT FANCY STUFF WAS THE SAME OLD LOCK. I TOOK THE LAST TWO NUMBERS.

THE COLONEL OKed MY REPORT, PUT IT IN THE SAFE AND LOCKED IT UP.

IT'S FINE.

CLANG

THE WAY YOU CLOSE THAT, I GET THE IDEA YOU THINK THINGS ARE SAFE IN THERE.

WHAT DO YOU MEAN? DO YOU MEAN IT'S **NOT** SAFE?!

A GOOD SAFECRACKER COULD OPEN THAT THING IN THIRTY MINUTES.

YOU CAN OPEN THIS SAFE IN **THIRTY MINUTES**?

I SAID A GOOD SAFECRACKER. IT WOULD TAKE ME ABOUT FORTY-FIVE

WELL! MY WIFE IS WAITING AT HOME FOR ME WITH SUPPER, BUT I'M GOING TO SIT DOWN RIGHT HERE. YOU'RE GOING TO WORK ON THAT **DAMN THING** FOR **FORTY-FIVE MINUTES** AND **NOT** OPEN IT!

I TURNED THE COMBINATION WHEEL AT RANDOM, JUST TO MAKE SOME ACTION.

THESE MILITARY GUYS...

EVEN FIVE MINUTES IS A LONG TIME WHEN YOU'RE JUST SITTING AND WAITING...

WELL? ARE YOU MAKING ANY **PROGRESS?**

WHAT DO YOU MEAN, "PROGRESS"? WITH A THING LIKE THIS, YOU EITHER OPEN IT OR YOU DON'T.

THEN I BEGAN TO WORK IN EARNEST AND IN ABOUT **TWO** MINUTES...

CLICK

I TOLD THE **COLONEL** HOW I DID IT, AND ABOUT THE **DANGER** OF LEAVING THE DOORS **OPEN** SO ANYBODY COULD PICK OFF THE LAST TWO NUMBERS. HIS SOLUTION?

```
Attn: All Oak Ridge personnel
Re: Possible security breach

If Mr. Feynman has at any time been in your office, or near your
office, or walking through your office, please change the
combination of your safe.
```

SO THAT WAS IT : **I** WAS THE **DANGER**. IT'S A PAIN IN THE NECK TO REMEMBER A NEW COMBINATION. THE NEXT TIME I VISITED, **NOBODY** WAS HAPPY TO SEE ME.

CONTINUED...

IN 1982, RICHARD FEYNMAN (RACONTEUR, ARTIST) AND TOM VAN SANT (ARTIST, RACONTEUR) FIND THEMSELVES IN GENEVA WITH TIME ON THEIR HANDS.

OK, WE'VE DONE THE SHOPS AND THE COUNTRYSIDE. NOW WHAT?

IF IT ISN'T TOO MUCH LIKE A BUSMAN'S HOLIDAY, I'D LIKE TO GO OVER TO CERN*.

SURE. I WORKED THERE A FEW YEARS AGO. I'LL SHOW YOU AROUND.

*CERN: Centre Européan pour la Recherche Nucléaire- the European particle accelerator.

CERN!

CERN

CERN?

CERN!

69

...SO A COUPLE OF DAYS LATER I WAS TAKING A CAB, AND THE DRIVER RECOGNIZED ME FROM THE TV...

HE SAID, "BOY! YOUZ HAD A HAHD TIME. WHEN DEY AKSED YA TA EXPLAIN IN TREE MINUTES WHAT YA WON DA PRIZE FOAH?

"YA KNOW WHUT I WOULDA SEZ? I WOULD A SEZ:

"IF I COULD EXPLAIN IT IN TREE MINUTES, IT WOULDN'T BE WORTH DA NOBEL PRIZE!"

Notes and References

Rather than specific notes on specific stories, below you'll find an annotated list of books and CDs(!) by or about Richard Feynman. If you enjoyed this section you'll enjoy these too. The first (and best) seven are by Feynman himself.

The Art of Richard P. Feynman, compiled by Michelle Feynman, (Basel, Switzerland: Gordon and Breach Science Publishers SA, 1995). A collection of Feynman's artwork in an expensive but handsome edition.

The Character of Physical Law, (Cambridge, MA: The M.I.T. Press, 1965). Beautiful lectures on why the world works.

QED, (Princeton, NJ: Princeton University Press, 1985). The best popular physics book I've read. It makes you think you understand Feynman's Nobel Prize winning work almost as well as he did.

Safecracker Suite, sound recording by Ralph Leighton, 1988. A CD of Feynman playing drums and telling the safecracker story to Ralph Leighton. 69 minutes and 45 seconds of fun.

Six Easy Pieces, (Reading, MA: Addison-Wesley, 1995). Feynman gives six of his most accessible lectures on the basics of physics. You can also get cassettes or CDs and hear it as if you were in class — with your eyes closed, anyway. Though the first lecture is difficult to hear because the source tape is in bad shape, until the films get transferred to videotape these CDs will remain the most accessible way to learn directly from the master.

"Surely you're joking, Mr. Feynman!", as told to Ralph Leighton, (NY: W.W. Norton, 1985). The book that made Feynman into the pop culture icon he is. Every story he tells entertains, and a few even enlighten.

"What do you care what other people think?", as told to Ralph Leighton, (NY: W.W. Norton, 1988). This provided the basic narrative for "Arline". It also covers Feynman's last public adventure, the Challenger inquiry. Almost as good as *"Surely you're joking..."*.

"Most of the Good Stuff", edited by Laurie M. Brown and John S. Rigden, (NY: American Institute of Physics, 1993). More anecdotes, including Danny Hillis' story, which originally appeared in the February, 1989 issue of *Physics Today*.

Genius, by James Gleick, (NY: Pantheon Books, 1992). Gleick has written an accessible biography of Feynman. He draws heavily from *"Surely you're joking..."* and *"What do you care..."*, but adds some context to their stories.

Tuva or Bust!, by Ralph Leighton, (NY: W.W. Norton, 1991). There's that Ralph Leighton fellow again. Not only did he do the "as told to" honors for many of the books listed above, he also gave his kind permission to adapt many of the stories you've just read. He has also founded an organization called the Friends of Tuva, dedicated to celebrating Richard Feynman's spirit of adventure. You can contact the Friends via email at fot@lafn.org or at Friends of Tuva, Box 70021, Pasadena, CA 91117.

The Beat of a Different Drum, by Jagdish Mehra, (Oxford: Clarendon Press, 1994). Another biography, this time by a colleague. If you choose to skip the hard technical parts (I certainly did) you may prefer it to Gleick's.

No Ordinary Genius, by Christopher Sykes, (NY: William Norton & Company, 1994). Tom Van Sant's CERN story appears in this well illustrated book in which many famous people offer their perspectives on Feynman — and their Feynman stories. Like stories about Jack Kirby (whose work inspired generations of cartoonists and scientists alike), it seems everybody has one except me.

Artists

Mark Badger has drawn books for DC, Paradox, Caliber, Marvel, and, well, you get the idea. Visit him on the web at *www.lemoncustard.com*.

David Lasky writes and draws *Boom Boom*, available from MU/Aeon Press, and has other projects in the works from the "Labor of Love" group.

Scott Saavedra writes and draws *Dr. Radium, Man of Science* and *Java Town*, published by the ubiquitous Slave Labor Graphics.

Rob Walton writes and draws *Ragmop*, published both by Image and his very own Planet Lucy Press.

...reading about it. So I told 'em I think I've developed myxoid liposarcoma, and I figure I only have an 11% chance of surviving 5 years.

The doctors looked at me like I was crazy!

Who the hell was I to tell them what was likely to happen to me?!

I said, "If I can't figure out my probable path*, I dunno who can."

heh heh heh heh

*Feynman developed path integrals as a powerful tool for doing quantum electrodynamics.

heh.

Hey, what's the matter?

77

...

I'm sad because you're going to die.

- sigh -

Yeah, that bugs me sometimes too. But not as much as you think.

Ya see, when you get as old as me, you realize that you've told most of the good stuff you know to other people anyway.

Hey! I bet I can show you a better way home.

And so he did...

SCIENCE

SAFECRACKER

PART THREE: TICKLING THE DRAGON'S TAIL.

THERE WAS ONE LOCK AT LOS ALAMOS THAT I WANTED TO CRACK MOST OF ALL...

COME ON, TRINA. YOU GOTTA LET ME. I'LL TAKE YOU TO THE **PX** TONIGHT **PLEASE** I'LL NEVER ARGUE ABOUT AN OVERDUE BOOK AGAIN PRETTY PLEASE--

GEEZ, STOP WHINING...

...I'LL GIVE YOU FIVE MINUTES THEN YOU'RE **OUT OF HERE!**

OKAY!

CLICK.

⚡#%☠🐛!

FINISHED, DICK?

HEH.

I NEVER DID FIGURE OUT HOW IT WORKED. IT WAS WAY BEYOND MY CAPACITY.

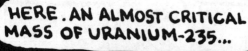

HERE. AN ALMOST CRITICAL MASS OF URANIUM-235...

...ANOTHER PIECE OF URANIUM, JUST LARGE ENOUGH TO MAKE THE WHOLE THING CRITICAL...

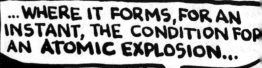

...READY TO FALL THROUGH THE **CENTER**, GUIDED BY THOSE RODS...

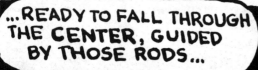

...WHERE IT FORMS, FOR AN INSTANT, THE CONDITION FOR AN **ATOMIC EXPLOSION**...

...WHICH WE MEASURE.

READY?

A-OK
YES, SIR!
HAI. YEAH.
DA. HA.

CLICK

CLICK

CLICK

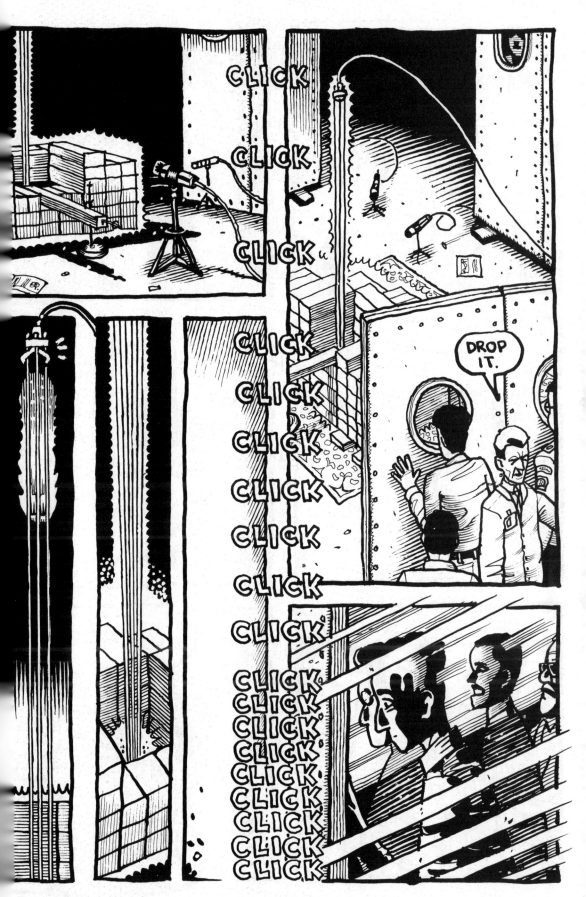

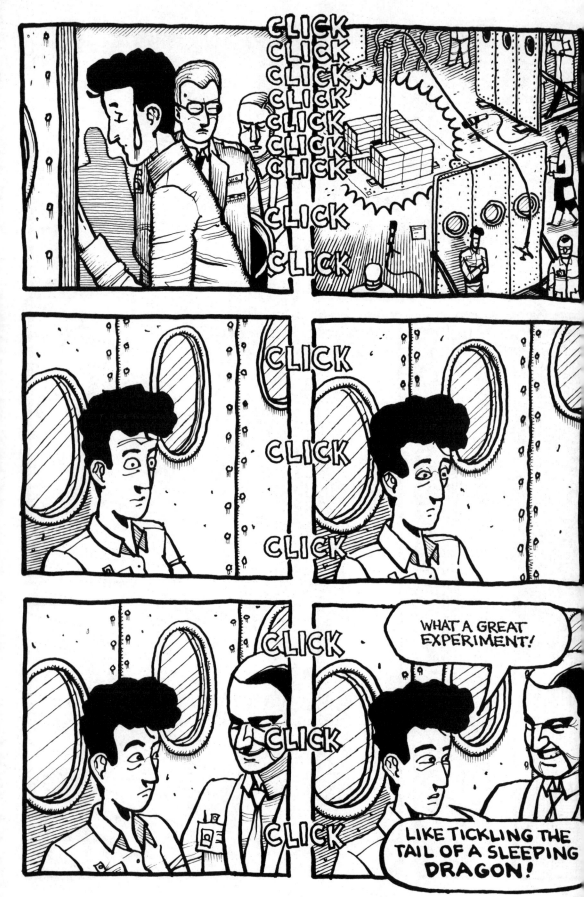

SO, CAN YOU GET YOUR KIDS TO DO THE CALCULATIONS BY THE END OF THE WEEK?

LET'S GO SEE.

THIS IS OUR "SPECIAL ENGINEER DETACHMENT."

HIGH SCHOOL BOYS WITH ENGINEERING ABILITY.

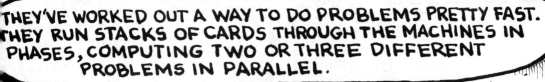

THEY'VE WORKED OUT A WAY TO DO PROBLEMS PRETTY FAST. THEY RUN STACKS OF CARDS THROUGH THE MACHINES IN PHASES, COMPUTING TWO OR THREE DIFFERENT PROBLEMS IN PARALLEL.

WE NEED THE CRITICALITY CALCULATION SOON.

CAN THEY DO IT?

GUYS! OTTO NEEDS HIS NUMBERS CRUNCHED FAST! WE'LL HAVE TO DROP EVERYTHING ELSE TO FOCUS ON IT.

WE'LL TRY IT!

I KNEW THEY'D SAY THAT, THEY'LL START RIGHT AWAY.

OK! SEE YA LATER. AND THANKS!

I HAD TO GO TO THE LIBRARY TO GET WHAT WE NEEDED TO DO THE CALCULATION.

LIBRARY CLOSED

MP

MP

UH-OH.

I CAN'T GET IN... AND MY GUYS WORK SO FAST THAT I'LL NEED THAT STUFF TONIGHT.

HEY! FREDDY de HOFFMAN HAS WHAT I NEED IN DECLASSIFICATION!

HOPE HE'S THERE.

HE WAS OUT.

I DIDN'T KNOW HIS COMBINATION, SO I THOUGHT I'D TRY OPENING THEM "BY THE BOOK". I'D NEVER TRIED THE OFFICIAL WAY BEFORE.

FIRST, THE SECRETARY: "SHE'S AFRAID SHE'LL FORGET THE COMBINATION, SO SHE WRITES IT DOWN."

I HAD READ THAT WHEN SOMEONE IS BADLY SCARED, THEIR FACE BECOMES SALLOW.

...WELL, IT'S TRUE.

HIS FACE TURNED A SORT OF GRAY-YELLOW/GREEN. IT WAS FRIGHTENING TO SEE.

"WHEN ALL THE COMBINATIONS ARE THE SAME, ONE IS NO HARDER TO OPEN THAN THE OTHER — THE SAME GUY."

FREDDY! WHAT'S WRONG?

L-L-LOOK AT THIS!

WHAT DOES IT MEAN?

ALL THE C-C-COMBINATIONS OF MY SAFES ARE THE SAME!

THAT AIN'T SUCH A GOOD IDEA.

I KNOW THAT NOW!

AND HE SIGNED WHO IT WAS! HE SIGNED WHO IT WAS!

WHAT?

IT'S THE SAME GUY WHO'S BEEN TRYING TO GET INTO BUILDING OMEGA!

"THIS ONE WAS NO HARDER TO OPEN THAN THE OTHER ONE—WISE GUY."

OH NO!

I'M GONNA GET MY THROAT CUT WHEN HE GETS TO THAT FIRST CABINET!

OH GOD!

OH GOD!

94

I'D BETTER GET THIS DOCUMENT TO THE GUYS, AND THEN GET THE HELL OUT OF HERE BEFORE FREDDY FINDS ME!

HEY, WHY ALL THE CARDS?

YOU'RE NOT SUPPOSED TO DO MORE THAN ONE PROBLEM!

ONLY ONE PROBLEM!

GET OUT! WE'LL EXPLAIN LATER.

SNATCH!

C-10

YOU KNOW HOW IT IS: THEY MUST'VE HAD TROUBLE WITH THE CALCULATION AND FIGURED OUT A WAY TO FIX IT...

F-FREDDY!

IT WAS YOU.

...THEN THE BOSS COMES WALKING UP...

JIM OTTAVIANI

T
H E N D

BEM 96.

96

1944:

After the German invasion, the U.S. Lend-Lease program sent critical aid to the USSR, who received 13,000,000 pairs of winter boots, 5,000,000 tons of food, 2,000 locomotives, and more...

The aid came on transport ships, by aircraft, and in diplomatic pouches. It was all freely given to our wartime ally...all except the atomic secrets stolen by Klaus Fuchs, Harry Gold, and other American spies!!

Every leg of that covert journey was perilous, as Anatoli Alexandrov learns when he tries to find his way to...

MOSCOW LAB NO. 2

STORY- JIM OTTAVIANI ART- LINT LUCAS

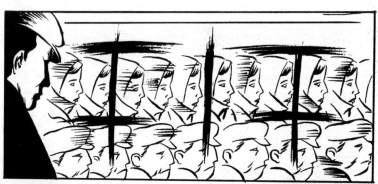

YEAH SURE...

IT'S OVER THE FENCE WHERE THEY'RE MAKING THE ATOMIC BOMB.

PERHAPS THERE ARE.

BUT IT IS DIFFICULT TO TALK SCIENCE WITH THESE NAZIS ALL AROUND US.

I SEE ONLY GERMAN SOLDIERS.

YES. THAT MAY WELL BE TRUE IN THE ABSTRACT...

THIS ROOM BRINGS BACK MEMORIES

WE DIDN'T ALWAYS DO OUR BEST WORK IN FRONT OF A BOARD

...CORPUSCLE AND A WAVE.

SO THEN NEWTON AND HOOKE WERE BOTH CORRECT ABOUT LIGHT!

YES. A PERFECT EXAMPLE OF A GREAT TRUTH WHOSE EXACT OPPOSITE IS ALSO A GREAT TRUTH!

TEN, THE NEXT DAY, WHAT WE SCUSSED ACTUALLY TURNED OUT BE CORRECT.

GET UP WERNER WE PICK UP SCHRÖDINGER THIS MORNING.

DR. SCHRÖDINGER. SO GOOD TO SEE YOU.

YOUNG WERNER AND I WERE JUST TALKING ABOUT THE WAVE NATURE OF LIGHT AND MATTER

YOU MUST TELL US WHAT YOU THINK OF THE QUANTUM.

ERWIN WASTED NO TIME, DID HE?

YOU SURELY MUST UNDERSTAND, BOHR, THAT THE IDEA OF QUANTUM JUMPS LEADS TO NONSENSE.

WHERE IS AN ELECTRON WHILE IT'S JUMPING? IT'S SIMPLY NONSENSE!

YES, IN WHAT YOU SAY YOU ARE COMPLETELY RIGHT.

BUT YOU ARE NOT THINKING, YOU ARE JUST BEING LOGICAL.

YOU SEE, THAT DOESN'T **PROVE** THERE ARE NO QUANTUM JUMPS. ONLY THAT WE CAN'T VISUALIZE THEM.

OUR CONCEPTS, WHICH WE BASE ON DIRECT EXPERIENCE, DO NOT APPLY TO THEM.

I DON'T WANT TO DISCUSS THE PHILOS OF THE FORMATION OF CONCEPTS.

...I *KAFF:* SIMPLY WANT TO KNOW WHAT HAPPENS IN AN ATOM...

...AND MY THEORY OF CONTINUOUS WAVE-LIKE BEHAVIOR MAKES YOUR CONTRADICTIONS DISAPPEAR...

YOU WERE SO DETERMINED, PROFESSOR, THAT YOU DROVE ERWIN TO HIS SICKBED,

NO! THEY DON'T DISAPPEAR, BUT SIMPLY SHIFT TO ANOTHER PLACE.

WHAT ABOUT EINSTEIN'S PHOTOELECTRIC EFFECT?

WELL, I...

WE INSISTED FANATICALLY AND WITH ALMOST TERRIFYING RELENTLESSNESS ON COMPLETE CLARITY.

AND COMPTON'S ELECTRON SCATTERING EXPERIMENTS? CERT...

NIELS.

AND PLANCK'S RADIATION FORMULA?

I DON'T INTEND TO CRITICIZE, IT'S ONLY TO LEARN THAT I ASK!

=SLAM=

WE SEE THE JUMPS DIRECTLY IN SCINTILLATION SCREENS. IN CLOUD CHAMBERS.

YOU CAN'T SIMPLY WAVE THEM AWAY AS IF THEY DIDN'T EXIST!

IF WE HAVE *koff* TO PUT UP WITH THESE DAMN QUANTUM JUMPS, I'M SORRY I HAD ANYTHING TO DO WITH IT!

BUT SURELY YOU MUST SEE THE REST OF US ARE VERY THANKFUL FOR IT.

I COULDN'T BELIEVE IT WHEN HE LATER WROTE AN ORNATE LETTER OF THANKS FOR YOUR HOSPITALITY!

HE DID, DIDN'T HE WERNER? AN UNFORGETTABLE EXPERIENCE FOR US ALL.

GET UP PROFESSOR! EINSTEIN HAS ISSUED ANOTHER CHALLENGE!

AS WERE THE SOLVAY CONFERENCES. I REMEMBER 1930'S MEETING AS IF IT WERE YESTERDAY.

EINSTEIN AND HIS GROUP CHALLENGE OUR THEORIES TIME AND AGAIN.

YOU WERE ALWAYS CONFIDENT, THOUGH I WOULD WORRY.

BUT BY DINNERTIME WE WOULD FIND A SOLUTION.

TIME AND AGAIN THEY CAME TO US.

THE THOUGHT EXPERIMENTS THEY CHALLENGED US WITH BECAME MORE DIFFICULT.

NO. YOU'RE NOT THINKING YOU'RE JUST BEING LOGICAL.

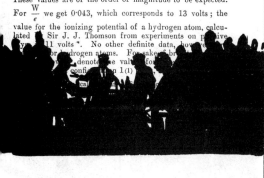

EACH TIME WE LED THE GROUP TO A SOLUTION.

For the permanent state of a neutral hydrogen atom we get from the formula (1) and (2) in § 2, putting F=1,

$$1_{(1)}. \quad a = \frac{h^2}{4\pi^2 e^2 m} = 0.55 \cdot 10^{-8}, \quad \omega = \frac{4\pi^2 e^4 m}{h^3} = 6.2 \cdot 10^{15},$$
$$W = \frac{2\pi^2 e^4 m}{h^2} = 2.0 \cdot 10^{-11}.$$

These values are of the order of magnitude to be expected. For $\frac{W}{e}$ we get 0.043, which corresponds to 13 volts; the value for the ionizing potential of a hydrogen atom, calculated by Sir J. J. Thomson from experiments on positive ... 11 volts *. No other definite data, howe... for ... drogen atoms. For sake... b... ... denote ... val... for confi... 1(1) ...

EINSTEIN'S LAST EFFORT WAS THE BEST.

HIS "CLOCK IN A BOX" THOUGHT EXPERIMENT DIRECTLY CHALLENGED YOUR UNCERTAINTY PRINCIPLE.

AND AGAIN, WE... YOU... PREVAILED.

DO YOU REALLY BELIEVE THAT GOD PLAYS DICE?

WERNER?

YES... AND NO. REMEMBER, PROFESSOR EINSTEIN:

THE ANCIENTS CAUTION US NOT TO ASCRIBE ATTRIBUTES TO PROVIDENCE IN ORDINARY LANGUAGE.

I WAS VERY PROUD OF YOU AT THAT CONFERENCE.

SO WHY DO YOU NOT PARTICIPATE IN THE CONFERENCES NOW?

LOOK AROUND YOU. WHAT DO YOU SEE?

WELL. THE NATIONAL SOCIALISTS DO NOT HONOR SCIENCE, SO THEY TREAT SCIENTISTS BADLY.

WHEN THEY ARE VICTORIOUS THEIR ATTITUDE WILL CHANGE.

AS THE RESULT OF YOUR NEUPFADFINDER MOVEMENT, I SUPPOSE.

NOW, YOU KNOW HOW I'VE ALWAYS FELT ABOUT NATIONAL SOCIALIST RHETORIC.

BUT I WILL TELL YOU WHAT I TOLD FERMI.

I FELT-- AND FEEL-- RESPONSIBLE TO THOSE YOUNG GERMANS.

AS YOU WERE TO ME, I MUST BE TO THEM.

PROFESSOR, COULD WE WALK THROUGH THE WOODS AS WE USED TO?

WE HAD MANY OF OUR BEST CONVERSATIONS THERE.

IF YOUR "SOLDIERS" WILL PERMIT IT.

NO PROBLEM, WE HAVE HALF AN HOUR. SHALL WE?

IF I LOOK AT THIS I WILL HAVE TO PASS WHAT I SEE ALONG TO THE ALLIES...

...REGARDLESS OF WHAT I BELIEVE ABOUT YOUR INTENT.

IF WHAT THIS PAPER SAYS IS TRUE, WHY DO YOU SHOW IT TO ME? WHO ARE YOU SHOWING THIS TO? YOUR FRIEND? A FELLOW SCIENTIST? OR A FELLOW SPY? I CANNOT... WILL NOT BE ALL OF THESE THINGS TO YOU.

IF IT IS FALSE, THEN YOU WOULD HAVE ME AS YOUR CONSPIRATOR IN PASSING THIS MIS-INFORMATION. HOW CAN YOU ASK ME TO DO THAT?

I

WE... MY GROUP... DOUBT THERE CAN BE FREE SCIENCE IN LIGHT OF A SUCCESSFUL ATOMIC BOMB.

VI ER MERE ENIGE END DE TROR...

WE'VE ALREADY LOST IT.

WE WILL EACH HAVE TO DECIDE HOW TO GO ABOUT GETTING IT BACK.

AND IT APPEARS OUR TIME TOGETHER HAS RUN OUT.

"VI ER MERE ENIGE END DE TROR." "IT APPEARS THAT YOU AND I ARE IN GREATER AGREEMENT THAN YOU THINK." A PHRASE BOHR WOULD USE WHEN HE THOUGHT THE SPEAKER WAS MISSING THE POINT ENTIRELY.

BOHR ESCAPED TO ENGLAND IN 1943. HE EVENTUALLY TRAVELLED TO THE U.S. AFTER THE BRITISH GOVERNMENT PLAYED HIM AS A TRUMP CARD TO GET INVOLVED WITH THE MANHATTAN PROJECT. HE LEFT EUROPE CONVINCED THAT GERMANY WAS ON ITS WAY TO AN ATOMIC WEAPON.

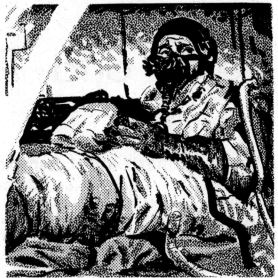

Niels Bohr, in transit to England.

Bohr and [John] Wheeler believed, correctly, that only a particularly rare variety of uranium could be used effectively in the creation of an atomic explosion. Bohr said this rare variety could not be separated from common uranium except by turning the country into a gigantic factory... Years later, when Bohr came to Los Alamos, I was prepared to say "You see..." but before I could open my mouth, he said: "You see, I told you it couldn't be done without turning the whole country into a factory. You have done just that."
— Edward Teller in THE LEGACY OF HIROSHIMA, (New York: Macmillan, 1962.)

HEISENBERG REMAINED IN GERMANY UP UNTIL THE SURRENDER. THE BRITISH REMOVED HIM TO ENGLAND AT THAT POINT, JUST BEFORE THE BOMBING OF HIROSHIMA.

Farm Hall, 1945: Heisenberg, held "at His Majesty's pleasure."

On the suggestion of the nuclear physicists we scuttled the project to develop an atomic bomb by autumn of 1942... It would have been impossible - given the strain on our economic resources - to have provided the materials, priorities, and technical workers.
—Albert Speer in INSIDE THE THIRD REICH, (New York: Macmillan, 1970.)

Notes and References

Russell Lectures on Cosmology

This version of the story appears in *A Brief History of Time*, by Stephen Hawking, (NY: Bantam, 1988), but the premise is much older. East Indian and Chinese mythology both have turtles standing in for the Greeks' Atlas, and Native American cosmology tells the story of Sky Woman: After she had fallen from a hole in the sky, three animals try to find earth under the waters to give her a place to rest, but only the turtle succeeds. Present day Iroquois call earth "Turtle Island".

Tickling the Dragon's Tail

See the notes for the previous chapter for a complete list of Feynman recommendations. But in addition, also read *What Little I Remember*, by Otto Frisch (London: Cambridge University Press, 1979) for the dragon's tail incident.

Moscow: Lab No. 2

Why the comic strip stuff? Two reasons. It adds a surreal touch — almost as surreal as Moscow must have seemed to Alexandrov as he lugged those stolen documents around. The other reason comes from a quote in *Dark Sun*, by Richard Rhodes, (NY: Simon & Schuster, 1995). David Greenglass' first thought upon finding out he was on the verge of being discovered as a Russian spy was "I'll never be able to read *Li'l Abner* again."

The featured strips are *Nancy*, by Ernie Bushmiller and *Li'l Abner*, by Al Capp. Some of the visual elements of the story come from Bernie Krigstein's famous "Master Race" from *Impact* #1 (EC Comics, 1955) and Harvey Kurtzman's "Atom Bomb Thief!" from *Weird Fantasy* #14 (EC, 1950). Other conscious nods to Kurtzman appear throughout this book, but many unconscious ones no doubt crept in: it's hard to tread new ground in comics because he was almost always there before you. He created *Mad*, where Wally Wood's parody of *Nancy* appeared. It's reprinted in Brian Walker's *The Best of Ernie Bushmiller's Nancy*, (Wilton, CT: Comicana Books, 1988)...as is Mark Newgarden's inspirational "Love's Savage Fury", which first appeared in *Raw*.

Heavy Water

You won't find the whole truth, and nothing but, in any of the following books. You didn't find it in the story you just read either. But in the course of working on it, I've come to believe that Bohr and Heisenberg interacted in much the way Steve and I have shown.

Uncertainty, by David C. Cassidy, (NY: W.H. Freeman, 1991). This book gives an in-depth biography of Heisenberg.

Schrödinger, by Walter Moore, (Cambridge: Cambridge University Press, 1989). Besides his amazing work on quantum physics, Schrödinger also made important contributions to the theories of color vision and biology.

Nazi Science: Myth, Truth, and the German Atomic Bomb, by Mark Walker, (NY: Plenum, 1995). Pretty scholarly and dry, despite the lurid title.

Niels Bohr's Times, in Physics, Philosophy, and Polity, by Abraham Pais, (Oxford: Oxford University Press, 1991). The definitive biography, written by a contemporary and peer.

The Making of the Atomic Bomb, by Richard Rhodes, (NY: Simon and Schuster, 1986). You'll have a hard time finding a better book about the subject than this. Not only is it meticulously researched, it reads like a well-plotted novel.

Niels Bohr: A Centenary Volume, edited by A.P. French and P.J. Kennedy, (Cambridge, MA: Harvard University Press, 1985). A beautiful book, covering many facets of this famous man.

Heisenberg's War: The Secret History of the German Bomb, by Thomas Powers, (NY: Alfred A. Knopf, 1993). More on Heisenberg's WWII experience, or as much as we can infer from the many conflicting accounts he, and others, gave.

The Night After

From a story told by Richard (him again) Feynman in *Six Easy Pieces*. Rose and Hans Bethe eventually married.

Artists

Colleen Doran writes and draws *A Distant Soil*, available from both Aria Press and Image Comics.

Steve Lieber has drawn books for DC, Paradox, Caliber, Marvel, and, well, you get the idea.

Lin Lucas' work also appears in *Top Shelf*, and if there's any justice his feature *Creepy Joe* will soon appear in stores near you.

The original reason to start the project which I had, which was that the Germans were a danger, started me off on a process of action which was to try to develop this system, first at Princeton, and then at Los Alamos, to try to make the bomb work: all kinds of attempts to redesign it (to make it a "worse" bomb, if you like), and we were working all this time to see if we could make it go. It was a project on which we worked very, very hard, all cooperating together, and with any project like that you continue to try to get success, having decided to do it. But what I did immorally, I would say, was not to remember the reason that I said I was doing it, so that when the reason changed — Germany was defeated — not the singlest thought came to my mind about that — that now I have to reconsider why am I continuing to do this. I simply didn't think...

— Richard P. Feynman, from *No Ordinary Genius*.

epilogue

IN 1938, HANS BETHE
DISCOVERED
HOW STARS
SHINE.

WE STILL DON'T KNOW WHY THEY'RE PRETTY.

30 VII 96